COVER PHOTO

The Columbus Lighthouse in Santo Domingo is one of the two sites claiming to hold the remains of Christopher Columbus. Although Columbus was initially buried in Valladolid's Spanish city, his son sent his remains to a monastery in Seville, Spain. The remains were later shipped to the Dominican Republic and then moved to a cathedral in Havana, Cuba. Columbus' remains were relocated again to a tomb in the Seville Cathedral. However, bones later found at the Cathedral of Santa Maria la Menor in the Dominican Republic were assumed to have been Christopher Columbus's remains. Without evidence of who the bones belonged to, the Columbus Lighthouse was built in honor of the great explorer.

Photo Attribution: 53874000 © Maciej Czekajewski | Dreamstime.com

COUNTRY JUMPER in the Dominican Republic,
copyright © 2020

All rights reserved. No part of this book may be used or reproduced in any manner whatsoever without written permission, except in the case of reprints in the context of review.

Contact Author at:
countryjumperbooks@gmail.com

Hello boys and girls! Do you know how many countries are in the world today? The answer will depend a lot on how a "country" is defined. Some countries are members of the United Nations, others are not, and some are given only partial recognition. However, they are just as important to learn about. Which country do you live in?

My name is COUNTRY JUMPER, and I'd like you to come and jump with me around the world. I've selected 205 countries to visit, so put on your Jumping Shoes and buckle up. Today we are visiting the Dominican Republic, a country in the continent of North America.

Table of Contents

Chapter 1: Facts

Chapter 2: Terrain and Climate

Chapter 3: Politics

Chapter 4: Education

Chapter 5: Transportation

Chapter 6: Holidays and Festivals

Chapter 7: Animal, Bird, and Flower

Chapter 8: Popular Foods

Chapter 9: Money

Chapter 10: Sports

Chapter 11: Music and Instruments

Chapter 12: Clothing

Chapter 13: Fun Places for Kids to Visit

Chapter 14: Other Interesting Facts

Facts About the
Dominican Republic

The Dominican Republic is a nation on the island of Hispaniola and is also part of the Greater Antilles island chain in the Caribbean Sea. Hispaniola was once divided politically into the Republic of Haiti (west) and the Dominican Republic (east). The history of the Dominican Republic (formerly known as Santo Domingo) can be traced back to 600 AD, when the island's occupants were the Taino people, an Arawak-speaking indigenous tribe. Christopher Columbus landed on the island on his first voyage in 1492, and it soon became the first permanent European settlement in the Americas. The town of Santo Domingo was built in 1496, and it became the new capital. During the 16th Century, hundreds of thousands of Tainos on the island were enslaved to work in gold mines. African slaves were also brought to the area in 1503 when the Taino population decreased due to disease, famine, forced labor, and mass killings. The African slaves' servitude was so harsh that they rebelled in 1522, which is recorded as the first Slave Rebellion in the Americas. French control of the western portion of Hispaniola was confirmed in 1697, and the 1795 Treaty of Basel gave France full control of Hispaniola. The abolition of slavery began in the Dominican Republic in 1801. The Dominican Republic was returned to Spain in 1814 under the Treaty of Paris. However, Haiti captured the eastern portion of the Dominican Republic in 1822, uniting all Hispaniola under Haitian rule. The Spanish-speaking inhabitants of the east region rebelled against the Haitians and proclaimed their independence in 1844. After three centuries of Spanish colonization, with periods of French and Haitian rule, the Dominican Republic was finally independent. The capital of the Dominican Republic is Santo Domingo. The population of the country in mid-2020 was around 10,848,000.

The official flag of the Dominican Republic was adopted on November 6, 1844. It was designed by Juan Pablo Duarte, who was an activist, a writer, a politician, and a military leader. The country's national coat of arms is featured on the flag. The blue on the flag stands for liberty, the white cross is a symbol of salvation, and red represents the blood lost by the nation's heroes. The Dominican Republic civil ensign also has the same design, but without the coat of arms in the middle.

The Dominican Republic's coat of arms was adopted on November 6, 1844. It features a shield with a laurel branch on the left and a palm leaf to the right. Above the shield is a blue ribbon displaying the country's national motto: Dios, Patria, Libertad (God, Homeland, Liberty). The words República Dominicana appear on a red ribbon below the shield. The shield's center has six spears, and there is also a Bible with a small golden cross above it.

A country's national coat of arms is a symbol that signifies an independent state in the form of a heraldic achievement. An important use for national coats of arms is as the main symbol on the cover of passports.

The majority language spoken in the Dominican Republic is Spanish. However, the local dialect is called Dominican Spanish. The basis of Dominican Spanish comes from the Andalusian and Canarian dialects, found in southern Spain. Dominican Spanish is a subset of Caribbean Spanish, and it also has some borrowed vocabularies from the Arawak language. Other languages include Chinese, Haitian Creole, Italian, Japanese, and Samana English.

In the Dominican Republic, the government supports the liberty and freedom of worship without any interference. Most worshipers are Christians, with the majority of followers claiming Roman Catholicism as their religion. The second most prevalent religion is Evangelism. Other religions include Atheism, Islam, Judaism, with a small community of Seventh Day Adventists, Baptists, Protestants, Mormons, and Jewish groups.

Image by Anne and David @ https://www.flickr.com/photos/annedavid2012/10828992273

Terrain and Climate of the Dominican Republic

The Dominican Republic has a complicated and rugged terrain. Four major mountain systems and three intervening lowlands exist in the east–west region. The country has warm and sunny conditions for most of the year. For this reason, the climate in the Dominican Republic is referred to as an endless summer. The country is located within the hurricane belt, and tropical storms are a major weather hazard.

Image by Ted Murphy @ https://www.flickr.com/photos/tedmurphy/3897267027

Politics of the Dominican Republic

The government in the Dominican Republic is classified as a representative democracy, where elected officials represent the people. The president functions as both the head of the government and head of a multi-party system and is elected for four years. The executive branch is the dominant branch, and the legislative branch consists of the House of Representatives (Senate and Chamber of Deputies). The Supreme Court of Justice exercises judicial power.

Image by Jean-Marc Astesana @ https://commons.wikimedia.org/w/index.php?curid=46079196

...tion in the ...can Republic

...Dominican Republic is organized in ... and the last year of preschool is compulsory. Primary school is mandatory for children ages six through 14. Secondary education caters to students 14 through 18 years old; however, it is not compulsory. Students receive a high school diploma after completing secondary schooling and may attend a university. Universities offer technical careers and undergraduate and graduate studies.

Autonomous University of Santo Domingo - Oldest University in the Americas
Image by Siso84 @ https://commons.wikimedia.org/w/index.php?curid= 2608914

Transportation in the Dominican Republic

The Dominican Republic has a modern and extensive public transportation system. Minivans are one of the cheapest ways to travel around the city; however, they are also the slowest means of getting around because they pick up and drop off customers along the route. Motorbike taxis are also popular among locals because they are inexpensive and fast. There is a metro train system with two main lines that are always being extended. Several international airports are in the Dominican Republic, and the Punta Cana International Airport is the leading airport.

Image by ORAD @ https://commons.wikimedia.org/w/index.php?curid=14625100

Holidays and Festivals in the Dominican Republic

The Christmas holiday is one of the most active and celebrated times in the Dominican Republic. Many Dominicans from around the world go back home to celebrate this holiday with family and friends. Due to the lack of fir trees in the country, charamicos are Dominican's Christmas trees that are handcrafted out of wood. On la noche buena (Christmas eve), Dominicans often gather for a big family feast and sing Christmas songs. They also attend midnight mass.

Image by Paul O'Garra @ https://www.flickr.com/photos/35138806@N08/30457316184

Carnival is a highly anticipated festival of the year in the Dominican Republic. It is celebrated throughout February and is the largest and most colorful event that has been going on since 1867. Festivities include going to parties, dancing in the street, participating in parades, eating and drinking, and wearing costumes. The costumes and masks are distinct to each area and reveal Dominican's folkloric traditions and beliefs. The most colorful event is the final National Carnival Parade, which brings together carnival groups and characters for one last time along the city's Malecón waterfront boulevard.

Animal, Bird, Plant of the Dominican Republic

The Dominican Republic has not declared a national animal. However, the country's wildlife includes the Hispaniolan solenodon, which is a nocturnal burrowing mammal that is one of only a few venomous mammals. Its toxic saliva carries the venom to its prey. This species of solenodon can only be found in Hispaniola and is considered endangered. It is described as having a long flexible snout, and it resembles a large shrew. They are nocturnal and are found living in forests and brush country.

Image by Seb az86556 @ https://commons.wikimedia.org/w/index.php?curid=15267645

The palmchat is one of the national birds of the Dominican Republic. The bird's name reflects its strong association with palms for feeding, roosting, and nesting. It is a small, long-tailed passerine bird. Passerine means that they have three forward-facing toes and one facing back so that they can perch easily. This small songbird is found in abundance in large groups. They sing and frequently squawk to communicate with each other. They typically nest on top of palm trees. The palmchat is olive-brown on top with brown streaks on its bottoms and has a large, yellow bill.

Image by Luis Alberto 9919 @ https://commons.wikimedia.org/w/index.php?curid=5684062

The Bayahíbe rose was declared the national flower of the Dominican Republic on July 12, 2011. The flower blooms from a rare cactus that is endemic to the country, and the plant resembles a shrub, reaching up to 20 feet high. The trunk is surrounded by groups of spines that erupt in bunches. Its leaves have a bright green color and are oval-shaped, and they bloom pink flowers. The Bayahíbe Rose Garden is the only place in the world where you can see this flower in abundance. It is critically endangered due to habitat loss.

Image by De Ymleon @ https://commons.wikimedia.org/w/index.php?curid=8646663

Popular Foods of the Dominican Republic

Dominican food is a mix of cultures and recipes with a unique personality. La bandera is one of the national dishes that consists of rice, red beans, and meat (chicken or pork) that is usually stewed or roasted. Its pungent tomato sauce is often derived from the combination of garlic, tomato, and green peppers. This colorful dish is a popular lunchtime meal that is often served alongside a salad.

Image by Richard Melton @ https://www.flickr.com/photos/53019927@N05/49666456111

Tostones are a popular Dominican food that holds a special place on the Dominican table. They are one of the many dishes that many of the Latin American countries share. Tostones are made from unripe plantains and served as a side dish with meat and fish dishes, or as part of a larger meal. These crispy delights are thinly flattened and salt-sprinkled before frying. Tostones can be served as an appetizer and served with a choice of dip like a flavorful garlic sauce. Tostones are also a popular street food that is sold at food stands.

Image by AMartiniouk @ https://commons.wikimedia.org/w/index.php?curid=33322378

Habichuelas con dulce, also known as sweet cream of beans, is a unique Dominican dessert. This popular dish is served each year during the Lenten period and is prepared in large quantities to share with family and neighbors. This is a rich, sweet cream made with slow-cooked beans, sweet potato, coconut, and sugar. Various spices, such as anise, cardamom, cloves, ginger, and nutmeg are added to give this dish a rich flavor. Once prepared, it can be garnished with cassava bread or cookies.

Money in the Dominican Republic

The Dominican peso (Code: DOP) is the currency of the Dominican Republic. It was first introduced in 1844 after the country gained independence from Haiti. The peso replaced the Haitian gourde. In 1905, the peso was replaced by the U.S. dollar. The peso oro coinage was first introduced in 1937, followed by paper money in 1947. In 2011, all banknotes dated 2011 and later were denominated in pesos dominicanos. Banknotes frequently used are 50, 100, 200, 500, 1000, 2000 pesos. Frequently used coins are in denominations of 1, 5, 10, 25 pesos.

Image by Hernan Bustelo @ https://www.flickr.com/photos/wanderlost63/7627732384

Sports in the Dominican Republic

Baseball is the most popular sport, and Major League Baseball has been recruiting players from the Dominican Republic since the 1960's. The country has the second-largest number of Major League Baseball players and stands second only to the United States. Another popular sport is cockfighting. Gambling on cockfights is part of the sport, which is conducted under a strict honor code. Other sports include basketball, golf, horseracing, soccer, and volleyball.

Music and Instruments of the Dominican Republic

There are many different categories of Dominican music, which is a result of the country's diverse population. However, the most popular musical genres are merengue and bachata. Other varieties of music heard in the country include Dominican jazz, rock, and dembow, a dancehall style of music. The Dominican Republic musical instruments are the güira, marimbula, and tambora (drum).

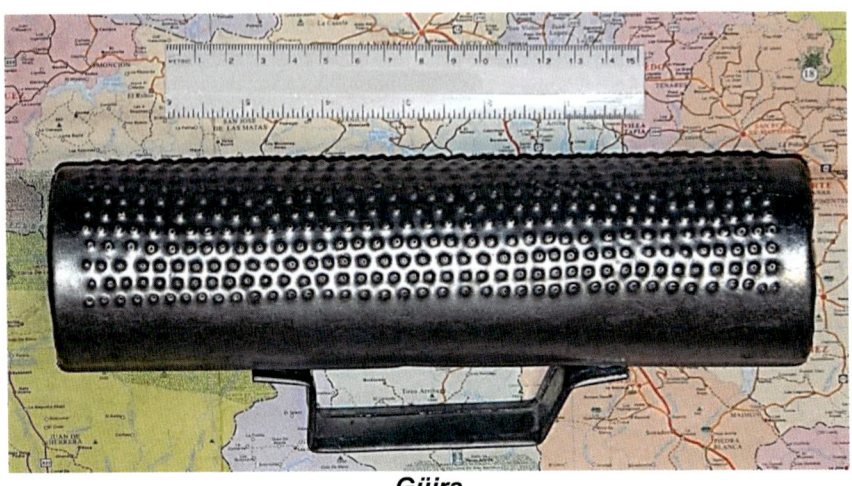

Güira
Image by Tim Ross @ https://commons.wikimedia.org/w/index.php?curid=3429411

Clothing in the Dominican Republic

Freed slaves in the Dominican Republic developed their own fashion statement to draw attention to their independent status. A distinctive Creole-style was created from the unique heritage of Arawak, Tiano, Spanish, African, and French traditions. Women in the Dominican Republic still wear this floor-length traditional dress. These colorful dresses often feature bright plaid or batik patterns and were originally meant to be worn on special occasions.

Traditional Outfit
Image by Mstyslav Chernov / CC BY-SA (https://creativecommons.org/licenses/by-sa/3.0)

Fun Places for Kids to Visit in the Dominican Republic

The Sirenis Water Park, located in the Punta Cana region, features water slides, a children's play area, kids' club, an infant area, and a large pool. Other attractions include a 10-meter high tower with two water tubes, two open toboggans, kamikaze, free fall twister, a themed Caribbean Pirates area for children ages four to 11 years old, four splash barrels, water jets, and sprinklers. This unique waterpark is located on the Grand Sirenis Punta Cana Resort.

Image by Steve Faulkner @ https://www.flickr.com/photos/108282727@N06/14198848194

Swimming with the dolphins is a memorable experience for visitors coming to the Dominican Republic. Dolphin Island Park off Bavaro beach, Dolphin Explorer in Punta Cana, and Ocean World Adventure Park in Puerto Plata are some of the locations to get a close-up look at these amazing sea animals. At the Ocean World Adventure Park, in addition to the dolphins, visitors can meet and greet sea lions, sharks, and stingrays. They also get an opportunity to pet and take photos with a trained sea lion, and jump into the water with sharks and stingrays if they are brave enough.

The Dominican Republic features 1,000 miles of white sandy coastline, making it the ideal climatic conditions for year-round sunshine and great trade winds for water sports. The Cabarete's Kite Beach is one of the most consistent places in the world for year-round kitesurfing. With a mixture of flat water and waves, there are many spots along the beach to choose from. It is also a great place for boogie boarding, surfing, and windsurfing. Instructors are on-hand to provide lessons to beginner, intermediate, and advanced participants. Other activities are also offered, including trips to waterfalls, canyoning, and diving.

Image by Christo Anestev from Pixabay

Other Interesting Facts About the Dominican Republic

- Before the formation of the Dominican Republic and Haiti, the island was jointly named Hispaniola.
- It is the second-largest island in the Caribbean.
- The Dominican Republic is the only country in the world to have an image of the Holy Bible on its flag.
- Voting is not permitted to the members of the armed forces and the national police.
- The Dominican Republic is the only place in the world where the blue, semi-precious stone called larimar is found.
- Coffee, sugar, and tobacco are the island's main sources of income.
- It is the most visited Caribbean destination.
- People of the country are loyal to their families.
- People of the island nation prefer living in joint families.
- The majority of women in the Dominican Republic have curly hair.
- It is illegal in the country to kiss a woman in front of a police officer.
- The people of the region are not known to be punctual.

That was a shortlist of only four countries beginning with the letter D. **East Timor** is the first country on the list of countries beginning with the letter E. The air travel distance between the Dominican Republic and **East Timor** is around 11,180 miles. It will take 19.96 long hours to travel between these two countries.

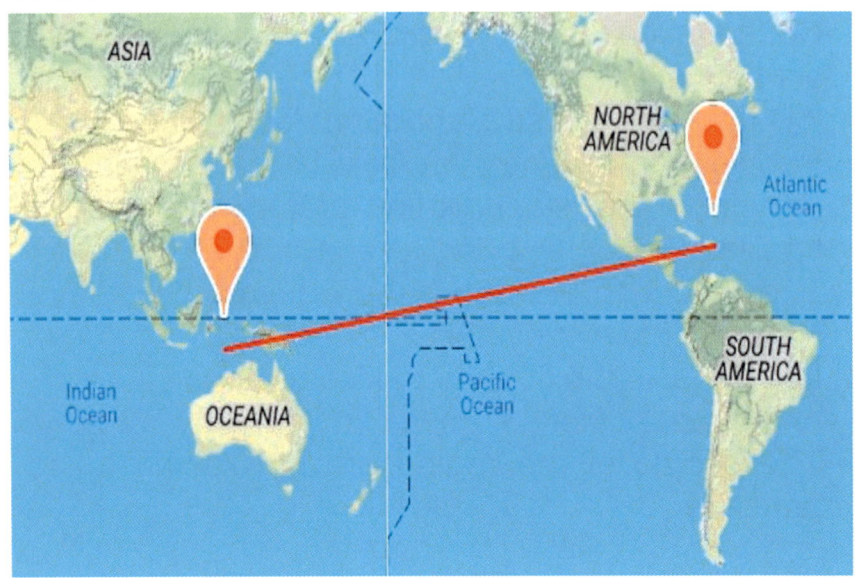

REFERENCES

1. https://slate.com/human-interest/2014/11/the-tombs-of-christopher-columbus-in-seville-and-santo-domingo.html
2. https://www.bbc.com/news/world-latin-america-19246340
3. https://en.wikipedia.org/wiki/Dominican_Republic
4. https://www.worldometers.info/world-population/dominican-republic-population
5. http://www.mapsopensource.com/images/dominica-map.gif
6. https://www.justlanded.com/english/Dominican-Republic/Dominican-Republic-Guide/Language/Languages-in-Dominican-Republic
7. http://kids.britannica.com/students/article/Dominican-Republic/274035/199708-toc
8. http://www.encyclopedia.com/places/latin-america-and-caribbean/caribbean-political-geography/dominican-republic
9. https://www.godominicanrepublic.com/travel-to-dr/getting-around-dr/
10. https://www.barcelo.com/pinandtravel/en/dominican-republic-christmas
11. https://www.godominicanrepublic.com/about-dr/carnival/
12. http://www.edgeofexistence.org/species/hispaniolan-solenodon/
13. https://www.reference.com/geography/national-animal-dominican-republic-e917edda1e1a49a9
14. https://saonadreamsweb.com/saona-island/the-bayahibe-rose/
15. https://www.donquijote.org/dominican-culture/traditions/food
16. https://www.dominicancooking.com/301-tostones-flattened-fried-plantains.html
17. https://www.dominicancooking.com/979-habichuelas-con-dulce-sweet-creamed-beans.html
18. https://en.wikipedia.org/wiki/Dominican_peso
19. http://exploredominicanrepublic.com/sports-in-the-dominican-republic
20. https://en.wikipedia.org/wiki/Sport_in_the_Dominican_Republic
21. https://www.thoughtco.com/music-of-the-dominican-republic-2141527
22. https://en.wikipedia.org/wiki/Category:Dominican_Republic_musical_instruments
23. https://kreolmagazine.com/travel-2/unique-creole-cultural-dress-of-dominican-republic/#.WdlvnmhSw2w
24. https://upload.wikimedia.org/wikipedia/commons/7/7c/Catalina_Island%2C_La_Romana%2C_Dominican_Republic._Men_and_women_in_traditional_clothes_are_performing_a_dance_under_bungalow_roof._%28reportage%29.jpg **[CLOTHING IMAGE]**
25. https://www.sirenishotels.com/en/punta-cana-hotels/grand-sirenis-punta-cana-resort/services/sirenis-aquagames-punta-cana/

26. https://www.familyvacationcritic.com/attraction/ocean-world-adventure-park/dominican-republic/
27. http://www.minitime.com/Gokite_Cabarete_Kiteboarding_School-Cabarete-Dominican_Republic-attraction
28. https://thefactfile.org/interesting-facts-dominican-republic/
29. https://www.distancefromto.net/distance-from-dominican-republic-to-east-timor

Continue following *COUNTRY JUMPER* as he treks across the globe from countries A through Z. Why stop here when there is so much more to learn about this great big world? Where will the next jump take you? You can follow *COUNTRY JUMPER* on his journey from A through Z or jump into the countries that you are curious to learn more about. A total of 205 books representing each country will be available in this series. If you cannot find a country that you would like to explore, please contact the author.

Happy reading!

Made in the USA
Coppell, TX
06 January 2022